T0120519

EMBER DAYS

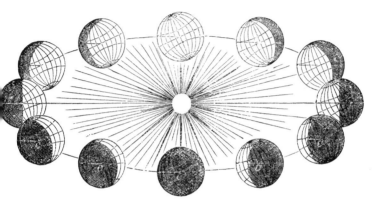

POETRY BY

MARY GILLILAND

CODHILL
PRESS

FURTHER PRAISE

Like the apothecarist Keats, Mary Gilliland's poetry wells up
from the healing force of unheard melodies. Her tensile lyric
and fluent narrative grasp the sweet otherness in life, which is
"Eve's radical helplessness" to endure and bear intimate witness
to both change and permanence....a radiant testimony—and
a triumph—of an unerring ear I deeply cherish. Mythical and
grounded, her sensuously rich language enacts a poetry in
which self-concentration brims beyond the far reach of desire,
passion, and the self.

—ISHION HUTCHINSON

By turns mystical and realist, Mary Gilliland's intensely musical
poems consider global apocalypse—"our course set for the
destitute sunset"—but also celebrate the generative power
of creativity, honoring the passion of cobbler, novelist, saint,
inventor, photographer. With preternatural empathy, she enters
fascinating sensibilities—Virginia Woolf, Nikola Tesla—and
sings "the troubled music" of history, a frontier that extends
from fabled to factual, from the Hesperides to the moon, from
resorts to war zones. Her vision is profound, enduring.

—ALICE FULTON

EMBER DAYS

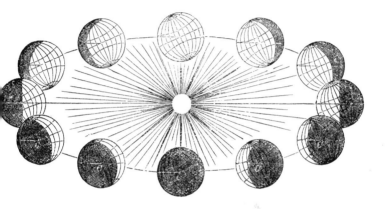

POETRY BY

MARY GILLILAND

CODHILL PRESS
NEW YORK • NEW PALTZ

CODHILL
PRESS

codhill.com

Published in the United States of America

ISBN 978-1-949933-19-2
Library of Congress Control Number: 2023937993

Cover and Book Design by Jana Potashnik
BAIRDesign • bairdesign.com

to Ellen Carr, midwife
and Michael Fitzgerald, iron welder
who traded the famine roads
of Mayo and Roscommon
for the row houses of Philadelphia:
ancestors

for my dear fellow poets who've exchanged our words about
each others'
especially the companion of my heart Peter Fortunato

CONTENTS

An Ember Week, built on earlier human observances of the sun's extremity at summer and winter solstice and the orb's pause at autumn and spring equinox, starts each season in the Christian liturgical calendar, traditionally observed with 3 days of fasting and prayer.

See Anglo-Saxon *ymbren*, a period, rotation, revolution.

Burn off my rusts and my deformity...

—John Donne

OFFERING THE BODY: THE TIBETAN PRACTICE OF CHÖD

The eagle does its day job
feasting on what's left by crow and vulture.
Anything I'd planned to do is over.

As my head nods its usual consent
to imaginary promises and dreams
my corpse appears before me.

Time's come to set my mind
to ribbon flesh, chop small, pile it in a dish
made from the cranial bones.

I scout the stinking ground for anything
to start the fire, use my own desire.
The skull cup, on its tripod, enlarges as it heats.

Half-moon on a finger
pokes from the pile of blood and bones
simmering to stew, to nectar.

All who are wise, the ordinary, furred,
obstructors, germs of sickness—
may their bodies, minds, be sated.

From every distance and dimension, beings
afraid, unsatisfied, or blessed, feast to satisfaction—
devils, angels, animals, everyone I owe.

I see no stopping to the world
but there is respite from the demons
that arise daily in the head.

>

That this ritual could do the same thing twice
—my awareness cuts that thought. O, I cherished
this poor body. I quake. Invite.

Now, knife the ritual words   *in vast space*
reduced to dust   mounded like clouds
clinging   dearly held   to let in silence.

For all that is perceived, flesh or consciousness,
appears then disappears, image in a mirror—
red drop, a fingernail, a ball of hair.

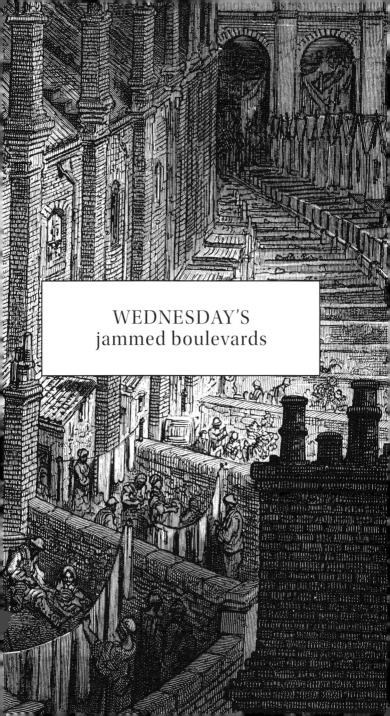

WEDNESDAY'S
jammed boulevards

INFINITIVES

To admit fields are on fire, oil fields,
though we do not yet see them burning;
to remember our grandparents sweltered
each summer, waiting for the streetcar,
for nightfall; to irrigate loosened earth
with native water; to bail out the seed
banks, to chew our food; to call the bluff
of the brand name, the marketing genius;
to digest resources burnt to a crisp threshold;
to savor our craving—to satiation;
to be free of litter strewn beyond us
steering through the Hesperides, sacred
groves, Blessèd Isles, past the ghost
of a man on the moon's new frontier,
our course set for the destitute sunset.

FOR WHEN NOTHING IS
REMEMBERED

On the eighth day we looked on and realized
it wasn't good anymore. Where did they go,
the shared rituals? We buy greeting cards
that could be sent to anyone, nineteenth
century fixtures shine without a lamplighter
and the city spent millions wiring
the whatnot.

Coffee in a paper cup, a painted wood duck,
little darlings on the back stairs fed
morning and night—no one born yesterday
will ever see contraptions that we use to
communicate. What of the game under
the tree root left behind the hill?
Step up.

And leave the affirmations by the wayside.
Inveigling all the separate types who
might begin to dance is no path of light.
Your hygienist can look for other work.
You might as well slink off to your room
without lipstick or a gold dress, seeds
in your hair.

THIS IS BUFF, SHUFFLING

The constant radiance of the nearer celestial bodies
gives the run to lumbago.

If you can't hear me I'll be in Ohio
past the rustbelt's easternmost snowbound city.

I can't blame my dead parents.

I'll walk about where the sky was when I first
opened my eyes. I'll castigate

the moon's and sun's rising and setting
as their inflammation

walks my white outline.

OUTSIDE THE TUNNEL
SNOW IS MELTING

Thank you, Mom, I found just
enough tablets to relieve
the worst symptoms.
Empty radiance or radiant emptiness—
why grouse about what's perfect?
This peacoat's already original sin.

Now it's just up these last steps
but after I unlock the door you better
go first. We have to make our way
through these stacks of boxes that came
down from the attic a few days ago.
Watch your knee on the newel post.

Born into the old blues, can't you
see what they've been doing
to me? with spiritualist church services
and one-liners written in hotel rooms.
How deceiving, the darkness.
The subtle capitulate, the young refuse.

I would have been a missing manual, blank
on the dusty flattened glove
you just picked from the parking lot
or the fluorescent lights
above the day-old bread
or the winter night itself.

You might have been duped by
serving evil or living for thrills
on the chance of one vulnerable moment.
Careful, that cup's chipped.
Here's a lace doily. No, password
has another meaning.

Can you preserve
the years in forty folders
fast and careless
as a transalpine express?
or coat the lawn with
genetic code or tragedy?

All these years you've been gathering
fruit at the end of a branch
I've spent time with the monks
incarnated this once as woman.
Do you know their cry
while flying? like ducks
with head colds.

See those ravens at eye level there?
and on the ground blacked-in
outlines cruise. We didn't
warm any else of it up.
Watch what happens
when what's happening
wants to stop.

EXCUSE ME HELLO
GOOD MORNING
GOOD NIGHT

Clear for days
the firmament masses cumulus
during the hour of eclipse
so the poppy-red medallion glides unseen
(jet fuel burns without our boarding)
and when the viewing time's elapsed the clouds disperse
doggedly as stage machinery
(with or without our purchase cows are sliced and packed)

A Bronze Star
pins the hero
a year after combat duty
while in *Newsweek*'s cover story his wife learns
(put 'waive fee' code into the system)
for the first time that bits
of bodies stuck like mud
(there is no charge for checks)

Please decline
sweets from strangers
if you hope to survive a cold war
or the iced globe after nuclear catastrophe
(how restrained, the oppressed, toward the West)
else the sun may set on
famous women, fair men and their progeny
(dictators unroll carpets of democracy)

'What is the shape
of the earth?—A pear!'—the wimpled
teacher's mouth waits not

>

hand chalking detail of the cell's mitochondria
(Pluto, Mr Pluto, do you hear us?)
and outlining the effects of sudden cold
upon the human kidney
(for we are nuns without the veil, and chemists)

UP WITH PEOPLE

I remember the opening salute, the hours
of taping and reshoot, our show's chief sponsor
Bab-O. I'd had to apply. It floors me now:

the ticked questionnaire on American
history, the patriotic essay I composed so
eagerly, a stalk among the standing waves of grain.

During commercial breaks for cleanser, I tended
my tender self-regard, inked in every anacrostic
in the book, won all spelling bees. Deadlines colder

than zero Kelvin in the outer regions before sleep
carried dust I could not fathom. Three. Two. One.
and camera rolled, the rest of the cast singing out.

They could not work me into their permanent
Youth Corps. Some they did, gathered at
the 30-year reunion, unbroken on the moving

belt of hearty cereal, furtive sex, and overtime.
I would have failed at reminiscing between
dances, blank on what I'd looked like, what I'd said.

KITCHEN THEATER

Make history pleasant; give it a changing
and half-slumped position. Make war
squat and cushion-like. Make a birthday
cake of the emperor's furniture—if a stick
persists, make warm brown tea. Aethelwold
is drunk again, Cnut buzzing like a fly.

Morning is a busy time. We must forget
variations on the quake and sweat
in a walk on the long stairway of necessity.

A great crisis occurred, guilty verdicts,
no rescue for the dead. Devoid of human
population, seas abound in fish. No such
seas are left. Put the project aside. No one
will miss you until lunch. History disappeared
in a yellow boat behind the island.

AS THOUGH FINNY FOLK
WOULD FLIP

As yet unknowing that fish
talk, ragamuffins living on the castoffs of the rich
believed the sound

was Russian sonar
or the CIA broadcast of operatives who spiked the Bay
Area's office Koolaid

rather than a feature
of the tête-a-têtes of simple fish whose school
colors matched the weathered

gray of houseboat hulls.
Echolalia—in those day—and echelons
were common.

In rank water
beneath the houseboats of Sausalito in the mid70s
plainfin midshipmen hummed.

Echolocation
was some imagined edge of language
for the experts

when anyone wo'th his salt
could hyphenate. In '75 you could nearly find Tallulah Bank-
head still alive

but no animal sound
was believed to signify—not dolphins, not elephants,
not—gadzooks and heck—

>

emissions of plainfin
midshipmen. It took a Cornell neurobiologist
who dined in gloves

in the lab building's
cafeteria sometime in the late 90s to determine
the source of the sound.

By her time
the houseboaters had stopped accusing anyone of spying
on their lives

for they had bottomed out.
They were renting basement studios. Ordinances
word processed skillfully

by cronies of the rich
had made the docks accessible only to other cronies.
At that time

and sometimes
even today, not all midshipmen are
commissioned.

SLIPPING AN OPINION
OUT OF THEM IS EASY

They've seen it all, been round the bend
and back. Is it my job to ensure answers
I record reflect their actual beliefs?
One guy claiming to be 'not denominational'
scored the perfect mean for liberal media reader.
I sense an emptiness in such respondents
although they maintain the mask of good
manners they bring to the landline.

Once there was a voice I could completely
give a body to, she was so well oiled, most
of her time probably spent at the marina
sailing her yacht into the fiercest wind in search
of a lungful with that old-time feel of
shock and grit. When I asked how she thought
she might survive the Rapture without smoking
she growled 'Can I swim in your pond?!'

ALL THOSE CREASES

If the source were a lily, if our
origin unfolded in a race of scent
strapped with color, then a technical
department would corner the research,
clip a petal.

            Cotton-mouth! Wool-gatherer!

If the end were lilies, if deepest
sleep folded steady as hills
miles from a fault-line, then a brace
of looters would sweep the carpet,
nip the fallen.

            Silk-witcher! Linen-lofter!

As we start nothing rises, nothing
withers as we finish; senses that
bring us drowned worms or harvested
stalks sense neither—this horizon
a field without

            puffy plants, downy beasts.

FROM THE WINDOW OF
THE PUBLIC LIBRARY

Like every town mine has budget-cut
the carousel down at the park
to make up for the federal shortfall.

A sudden gust of maturity shifted my retirement
to stocks. I am shivering and embarrassed
like a girl scout camper with glued hands.

'Where am I at, dear?' to anyone in the day room
with our bedsores and wrist restraints
I will chant above the lunch tray.

One of those milkweed pods set to explode!
Early on I learned who's boss, my eyes
clenched over alphabet soup.

THE OLD MAN BROUGHT HOME

My father once wore one shoe and one slipper
            pressing star moss and vole tracks
                    walking steep land

A stubbled saint fizzling in a twentieth century
            incarnation, afraid to use
                    the cellar stair

Or to digest the darkness that had been
            his middle age. He broke off
                    old branches.

As his hand brushed their papergreen lichens
            brittleness pleased a slender novelist
                    tossed inside

Who spoke to a cobbler bent over
            blue suede or white leather
                    at his bench.

NATIONAL INSECURITY

Curled and ready, she is the same age she always was,
red within slick darkness, cruising the doorman, her fate
to find herself never looking a bit lost, never the foreigner
at the airport. You kill me now, you really do!

Get lost, she thinks, *Queen and King of the Dwarves!*
as she waits in her ruined silk evening dress,
her ankle straps. Her bootlicking relatives lope about
to get things done. They forget to dust ceramic birds
on the windowsill, the traps in the basement.

That hobnailed stare! not a gaze—past leaves in dim
alleys of branch, growth burning green as stained glass.
Will they not notice the cabbie, the park? Stop to lie
on the grass, watch the gnats dance like bright dust?
They stick to the list of chores: chopped meat, detergent.

They'll hold their drinks like tickets to a new world
while, whiskers atwitch, mice queue at the baseboard.
Opinionated, she's quiet about it. Helicopters hover
the jammed boulevards, the old skyscrapers stand.

IF GOD WERE TO DIE

At least we would still have St. Nicholas.

You might say that memory depends on
whether we can hear each other but

during some urgent phone calls the receiver's
vacuuming. Santa's inside-out red sack

gone out of vogue shakes the hope that
academia will bluebook its merger

with Monsanto. From the corporate angle
all faiths equalize or at least isosceleze when

the average student argument posits
both Hitler and Darwin as examples.

'A lot of people who have a past
wind up here,' they say about the ex-cons

in Dubai. 'It's like a new Australia.'
You might say that we need rain

but do you want it? Whatever you say
at least a B. As you live and breathe you

lie down nightly. Can you kick up
those locked knees? Any use, the Russian proverb?

Hyperextension would help you stand
up to father but sorely strains the outer

leg muscles. Anyway he's gone now.

FEEDING IN FLIGHT
TO KEEP HOVERING

Through, I am through, being his old lady
—bug! He should rot in termite hell.

The war stories are flapping
from corners of my mouth
when with his rag the barkeep says
no more for you, sweetie.

I'll endure endurance—
with a voice you could use for jello.

This was to be my season in the sun!
like the periodical cicada.

Look, the barkeep says
when God talks to you
they say it's schizophrenia
but talk to God, it's prayer.

White gummy juice my chin may run.
I'll sit on this stool like a Buddha.

I leave my glass half-empty on the counter.
Outside I stare at mountains, roll the paper, lick.

The line of hills shifts, lifts.
A cocoon is hanging from that maple.
An airy moment's surely on its way.
I'll be strong now and exhale later.

STEALING ACROSS THE SILVER

A small firmament is turning on your finger as you rub its emeried surface, the embossed silvered bear. Your brute enjewels the universe—while someone else eases arthritis pain in four short weeks, bothers with hay fever.

Spare yourself a life of needlework and picnics, your scuttered hair permed alloy. Blood pressure screening may be free and confidential but try out the universe seen from afar—pale green.

Galaxies bailed out on their blue period eons ago. Astrophysicists average the spectrum of planets, stars, white dwarfs, black holes to a wavelength nearly turquoise.

What glints from bilious matter! and so distant across space. The yet more distant future average will resemble slaughtered meat, chapped lips, a face after a load of hiccups.

THE BOSS'S OPERATION

He sits at his desk, reads the paper,
talks to all comers, skips his sick days.
His lips pinken and puff, scrape his forehead

as the smile climbs out of his face.
One can always find a use for old parts
the script on his dull steel pate.

In the dark he does nothing
then he does it better. A grey blur
the boss, moving with skeletal patience.

Precedent precedent mutters his scalp.
If he would pillage, he must shun melodic

preludes, affordable appliances, speed
traps, recipes. Do the stars fear?

He's wide and wears big shirts, native
variety cramped to a specialty, his eyes
pools fixed in the sovereignty of his being.

Black gold pipes the seas and land,
flickers its promise
to ease pain and feed the hungry.

It's hard for cars to see him crossing
the road. He tucks in his tummy, ignores
the diagonal. He'll milk them for all they've got.

THERE IS NO KNOWN REMEDY
FOR SCALE

It twists leaves, embitters the life force.
Citrus whorls sooty, shade trees shine brown,
the dogwood goes scurfy with cottony dots,
ivy—of all spreading plants tenacious—
relaxes its air-borne roots, broken string.

Scale takes rose too, and lilac.

Egg-hatched or born live, the young sense stem fluid,
nectar, the span of a leaf, the redolent
venture. Each charts a spot, drops a mouth
for an anchor, the days incurable
staccato curves.

IS A TRANSCENDENTLY BEAUTIFUL PLACE NOT TO BE OURS?

The sea bangs about and sweeps out half the earth
of Isle Dernière, with half its 1856 summer residents.

Chance combinations of genes or plans based on
the weather consign personal fate to probability.

How many can rise to the side of the saints
and float among the rocks in a white dress?

Shifting winds sweep Emma Mille back in. Little bags
for keeping miracles streak her cheeks, lumps of fool's gold.

On the last barrier island, entranced, shivering
beneath the doctor's stethoscope, Emma fever dreams:

The great clod across the marsh channels
erodes with each storm strike. In the century

after steam, then the century after flight
mortals will rebuild, sight rocks to float among.

BLOSSOMS BURST EVERY-WHICH COLOR

When I took charge of the cemetery
the robin was in the rose—

nestlings with yellow-lined beaks
shoveled the air for food

a parent with worm perched the spit-woven
grass and twigs like a headstone

in the non-essential service of living
there was a frenzy of feeding

soldier-girl equal in combat was
finding her orderly way to a little nest

accordion-girl chirped her way
through another forced lesson

boy-girl was climbing the tree with
apples to eat the cyanide seeds

thorned were the corporate shoots and the banks'
fine roots and taproots in nations

thorned was the reach of anyone left
in the wake of commodities traders

the rose rambled with wrinkled
leaves, orange hips, a fragrance like cloves

the rose climbed six sunny feet
unbothered by pests or diseases

the rose rooted one with the fire
of doubling, hybridization, mutation

—of all birdsong the robin's
repeated one is most grating

and it rained so much all summer that I
mowed, mowed, mowed the lot under

FRIDAY'S
cash worthless

PERHAPS I LEFT THE CAR
AT BIG LOTS

My yard is limbo, rampaging beds
of succulents and stalks, a place for
the innocent, a palace of nonresolution,
its conundrum cross or crucifix—
the clean whistle of perpendicular boards
or the gallery of whispers
around the writhing figure,
the little piece of culinary art.

I have my own sadnesses, having reached
the end of my smoke rope and all my
excuses for lighting up—that it keep me pagan,
transcendental, strong and young, lit from within.
The telephone rings, mail arrives,
there are meetings to attend
and the list divides, clones, unfolds mercilessly
until, looking for the rake among leaves against

the slatted fence, I am convinced
that it was stolen by the cook
next door, traded for crack. Where is calm, peace,
absence of war? It's all bits, parts, fragments,
divisions, subdivisions—the brilliant
jay, the desperate squirrel, my neighbor in his
old Yankee cap sobbing by the garage
wall—I've found the keys. But I can't leave.

PAT EUPHORIA

~~after the Scottish National Gallery exhibit of Lee Miller's opus~~

How does a soul find its way from
the twenty-first century, a gold-
plated odeum with one in ten
scenarios to play, an October
palace of leisure with malice,
more people in pieces than
ever? It's too late to
slash my wrists but I know
why one would want to.

My feet have a tide, they go
numb and recede. How straightforward
the past, a land of carriages
and working farms, as though murder
skulked then only in high places.

Toes, oh the toes—can't touch broken
pebbles on the shoulder of the road,
imbibe the garden soil, the city
sense of tarmac. I lean
where the windshield
glass lodges. Hardheaded gal
I try to step back in.

If I could weight the rim
of my boot, wear down the heel,
crush the day's messages,
cracks in the sidewalk...

Lions and mice flatten the grass
and leave prints in dirt.
I no longer move
on anything softer than ice.

If I could call for
assistance, steal downtown
overland, lure a skyscraper toward me,
glide in for an afterhours massage...

On a heated slab
breath could stream, ribs spread
like an earthly walker's,
someone fondling my two lonely soles.

My ex remains a green man in the compost
round dome gleaming, wire rims licked
with grizzled curls. His cellar is well stocked;
vials I once would have traded a right
arm for are his discards. I sight him
passing in a fast car, slamming to a stop.
Brown bags wrinkle on the bucket seat:
the stripped corncobs, potato peels of youth.

Heart, I implore, after years of resentment
would you say we have somewhat in common?
Though I grew more like the owl,
mother of the birds, than like his peacock,
I could take on my own excess
without the flesh's fear
of being ridiculed or touched, and say
kindness itself would be enough.

In recurring dreams of travel
I tried to get not up but over
highways to a place to get away.

Departure time is pending and I'm
rolling scattered clothes, tickets
indecipherable, directions gone askew.

Miles of exhaust, blocks of exhale
unwalk the step of body
swapped to make myself a name.

There wasn't sweat to speak of, fingers hooked
on ten-pound weights. Nights of muscles
barbelled dumb would leave my mind
pocky as the mackerel-clouded sky.
Well-spoken women are flowers
blown on stone. The cull.

Above the city—ribbing, scales, sunlight cupping
pockets of the dark—a swart fish of the heavens
plies the line to the horizon. Swim, helpmate,
you'll surface to the name, the fame
glued to the guy beside—yours, the twilight.

Give your favors, you'll be thrown back anyway.
An easy mate to sleep with, you won't
rustle in the night, tired from the movement
that muscles haven't made.
Undone, cleaned as you were caught.

Three miles' stroll parallel the trolley
—mother's mother's constitutional
until the age of ninety-three.
Mother's suburban daily: two.

'Sister, what's this tendency
to torpor, stasis in a chair
with a book that wrecks the eyes.
Must be your father's branch, the guys.'

A superb day out she'd want me for:
bargains at the factory shop, tea rooms,
a free shuttle from one end of the mall.

What I wanted: native trees -
otters denned in riverbank -
ospreys free to breed, brood, hatch -
grazing that increases wildflowers.

What I wanted: water vole - mountain hare -
Atlantic salmon – pillwort - sticky catchfly.
What I wanted: movement that moved me.

I stretch arms don't feel a thing
Where's the hand   to hold   the handle
latch   car   door   —The picture's moving

Heaven's crystals falling
strike the road with a cold sting
blunt arrows on the worried guardrail

Death's a starter! the body a transparency life vaults
with the urge and sea of a first kiss
then all anyone becomes: song passed to another.

Seek buds and find flowers
Complete both sections of the form
Hardship makes the heart grow harder

Pruning amplifies air circulation
Talent levels with applause   Black ice forms
when temperatures near freezing

Seedlings harden off with time
Take one giant step   Three baby steps
Fasten safety belt   Adjust the mirror

The chance pass at entrance, cameo, or role
on Fleet or Wall or Easy
dots the declamations

Naivete obverts sophistication
Turn wheel in direction of the skid
Step light   Step back   Step out

I AM THE BLOND YOU WANTED

Hadn't you kept revving a green TR4 convertible
through the maze of Boston streets, and running
over hearts on breaks from basement sets during
our years apart? Your inking dots and hatches
far into the night has bent you like a crane.
Your jaw hangs open at odd moments although you
cannot sense it, meds that might or might not
have helped your soul leaning on the nerves. Still
good at stories, you don't track those already told.

To dream you, find you, phone, hear you paint
the North Atlantic's colors as you listen to it roll.
To tell you I see fireflies arc my dusky woodland
as the sawing shifts to cricket from cicada.
My eternal husband, your two ex-es. To while
our memories for hours, as we did making them afternoons
after school. Slap and ebb of journeys west but different years.
Your deep voice a corridor. Do I remember what we were
doing, alone in the house, while Light My Fire played?
You giggle. We decide to close the miles between us.

You walked last night from fireworks
into fireflies. We're softened now—
the middle, thigh. The last thing I expected
was a crew cut. Shoulders forward and arced neck
keep you ahead of me as we circle the pond
although our feet on the sidewalk move side by side.

I was a girl skipping stones at Salt Brook
who woke slowly, seized in a field, and you
raised me from my ancestors, my doubt and faith
and singular scholarship, my intact body.
I am the grown girl who knew you—nail-bitten,
side-burned, crotch bulging with honey—who

loved all that grunt and curdle, pursuit and
flight—although I did not fly. What keeps
my hand from your torn fingers? My hundred
take-me-back calls? Your one? waking me beside
the man I'd found, the bedroom like a rumpled
beach and last night's wrack washed up
and drying. Miles off, your reach, from the bucket
seat, sports car ceiling mussing up your hair.

DRY DOCK

That autumn afternoon
I brought the world into her room
—a tall and rustly spike—

the pale girl in the other bed
knew the past no more than I did
after three days in a dorm

>Unpacking, part of me discarded
>the nametag sewn in each collar
>and the major I had declared

>Toy gun sales and skirt lengths
>my teen editorials, mercurial
>men brokered genocide

>>I would lick the stamp on a blotter,
>>learn tuition and fees were funding
>>new ways to rain napalm

>>A dusky boy had me joy
>>in six coffees with milk
>>as we sat overlooking a lake

The main-—barnacles, bounding: yellow-green ooze
         flaking and gouged
                  Hull raised, bilge pumped, underside steady

Dotted and dashed; scrap and fragment: the hill steep, lumpy

That day yellow dock raised my soul
—the stalk ending in burnt-orange furls
tapped on my boot as I walked—

the Coke bottle's thick green glass
propped nature's spear on my desk
as I studied beyond the derivative

Rank weed, brittle spire; prized bloom, softened o'keefe

My grave severe ancestors risked so much to leave Ireland,
expected so little

The speckled fringed vulva I now afford water
parts thighs of air
with its green orchid stem

COMPARED TO WHAT WAS
IS IS BEAUTIFUL

the bread eaten, the westerlies
intuitively understood

lattice-blinds hanging askew

meander   deserter   maneuver
marching on but not over the tongue

the orchid's pouch gradually enlarging

bunchgrass stippled, light flexing
on rags hung to dry

1961 SPRINGFIELD AVE

After lemon-lime syrup and fizz
at the corner soda fountain
Linda Ambliss and I crossed the uncut grass
in a summer light free of mosquitos
daisies wheeling at our knees

There was nothing anyone could tell us

Halfway back from the walk downtown
where we'd face Betty and Veronica in the comics racks
we opened the front door of the abandoned house

The ivory wallpaper had wrinkled
above floor boards bare and wide

Inside on a table beneath bold-faced titles
in *The Delineator* of 1895, two columns of cramped words
sometimes parted for line drawings

—iron mattocks, curved ash handles
whalebone stays, silk seal plush capes
bitters for a lady's palpitations—

essential items to be ordered through the mail
none of which we'd seen in Miles Kimball catalogs
or on the rare city trip to Gimbels

Thanks to an engineer at Bell Labs up the hill
who'd insisted the transistor's
strength was its small size
there was a world that rock and roll was helping
us invent—through a wire in one ear

We sank with *The Delineator* on a sofa
to gaze at print in such proportions
that our histories of Hawai'i, Iceland, *Kon-Tiki*
and *Little Women* could have filled out
pages 1 through 150 in that catalog

I thumbed through Rickrack Samples
for the Seamstress, Mazurkas Scored for
Piano, Oxygen Home Remedies

I thought about young women who in 1895
began to queue for factory workshifts
instead of household service

the sofa not as soft as over Linda's
where we shrank before the flying saucers of
Way Out and I who was never left alone at home
to watch TV pretended comprehension
of *Tonight Show* jokes

Seated alphabetically beneath fluorescent lights
we'd recite Masefield's running tide
We'd chant one times one through twelve times twelve
and memorize by heart our catechism

We'd stroll by leveled limed lawns
each with a sapling
six feet from a new granite curb

to the library for Mrs. Proctor's patient tongue's
lick of a peony sticker, my 7th Summer Reader sheet
—almost done with Garden Flowers—

Almost in, 6:08: the whistling Erie-Lackawanna
bearing fathers who had all day checked
column totals for the sales of picture tubes

The Delineator advertised Chautauqua's Literary and Scientif-
ic circles, their 17th
Thomas Edison had wired their hotel

Linda rummaged through the desk's damp must
then squeezed the drawer back in its casing
I tapped floors for a trapdoor

We wanted clues about
someone—briefly absent?—who had filled the uncapped
inkwell to write the winter order:

—Tea, Spice, Baking Powder
Instructions for Point Lace
Doily Patterns, Dr Thomas' Complexion Soap—

The spray truck rumbled by, going to refill the tank with
DDT

Linda rasped to me *at night a girl can bleed*

The fountain pen was left upon the desk
There was a long staircase to ascend

Had she been incorrigible? ignored
the ads, absorbed sheet music? been made
to practice, practice until practice made perfect?

Had she with best friend walked about
—ten year olds believing in their nation—
on a vexed election night? had there hovered in the crisp
uncertain sky three saucers of light?

TO THE DARKHOUSE

Her exorbitant mind with
stood headache persistent as sea ur
chin spines.
But neural plasti
city went narcolept when con
catenations of spec
ular voices clung like electric
eels, nasty welts lodged in her cortex.
Her whole word family halted at the border:
the unspeakable splashed from its burrow,
stronger than she, lush rupture
of young body stilled, explored
as though she were a country.

Scratched reams of ink
have always brought me
the next novel's shape, its true begin.
Troweling through talk overheard
in a shop, on a corner, I carefully
brush stray tendrils, the toque,
cut of the jacket, length of the skirt,
crux of a character who finds herself
in a favorite chair, a room where she moves.

This site would not ex
cavate. It held sound
waves, no footing, the an
cient sea culling its sed
iment, a wet rush of grief
and release: his chat
tering teeth after climax,
her stifled bounds.
The day was overcast. After lunch
she'd smoke her two Sobranies,
let wraiths roam her palate,
then walk by the river, some
thing in her pocket besides hands.

THE GREAT BEAR IN WINTER

She's not fond. She sometimes
cuffs you down about four
when the shadows have stretched
your plans to ribbons.
It's not right; you roll up cranky
several hours later
lost in deep snow, you'll never make tracks.
She's gone to the sky. And you're stuck,
not content to luxuriate as
a furry ball, feeding on your own fat
with that winter gift—can they really
manage all season in hollow trees?
You envy her steadiness. She
shines in her kingdom and you know
she'll elude you all night.

TESLA ON A LEASH

You think the globe solid throughout,
cobalt, treasure blue, ramming its way
through galactic dust, life well used
and passive, what's termed everyday
satisfaction. Image the murky bottom,
thousands of tons of waste from the race
for the A-bomb. Make the land shift,
the seas hold. The sphere clears,
its path the smoked whirl of a catseye
skating parquet. The litterbag
needn't be emptied, there's so little in it.
                                        That would be science.

To be honest, nothing has fit since the
fields of Croatia vanished behind me,
the wheat in ribbed vaults, a cathedral.
Order and beauty—and that slight discrepancy:
leaving the homeland to find whether I
could come into my own. Years later my
mother was dying. From a coldwater
walk-up in lower Manhattan, I saw her
the way I see lines from the sun, grids of
power ensouling the planet we stand on.

Others seek greener grass, cloudier skies;
for me what fits is southern light: color
streaming though an arbor, striking a jaw hinge,
rankling earlobe and cheekbone, flushing
an entire face. The actual world is worth
all my appetites.
              When my patron Morgan realized
that sun as the endless free generator
would turn him no profit, when my no-further-

funding letter arrived, when I left
the electrical towers to dry in
the desert—wasn't that a cloudless day?
The train I boarded swallowed me
black and white, enlarged and dry-mounted.
Iron rails tensilled beneath iron wheels.

Morgan's wallet spilled hundreds
of households. His blueprint,
the future, entered by accident,
a breath floating by or a momentary
scent of rain: utility. Detrained in a
drab Eastern city, I chose a hotel
room and didn't come out. Daily I mumble,
forgoing the lightning and rod, repeating
the formulas, forcing my head to a
circle like everyone else's.

IRISH EYE

I don't have to hold my face on.

Where to begin? Liberal anti-clerical goings-on
every night of the week, especially sober?

A perpetual past beginning the future.

Cold nights crickets don't get to sing
so they rub legs all day in the grass.

Day after day being a carbuncle.

Sepia veers on laser printer.
A box of boxes. A bag of bags.

Grandmother's famished frown leans in recognition.

MIRACLE MILES

In the American tradition of realism
I do not live where I was born.
One self or another
I make as I go along.

I can cross paradise without my shadow
—a legal resident
permitted to swear in, swear out
—like helium—my presence.

I hear better in landscapes without deeper
meaning—ballparks, movies, restaurants—
than while I smoke next to the pump
when they refill my tank's vermillion.

It's hard to admit I convalesce
from my attempts to drive away
the natural sounding sounds
and the way the sun can set me.

BASE OF PARNASSUS

Down in the valley there's a levee
built against a flood of lazy sex.

The central story? Hanging at the old
mill, slogging along at the wheel

that makes cash worthless, entranced
by rotation. Bucket after bucket

rounds the top, spills—ker-plash!
the stream of desire: toiling drays, donkeys

slowly rising, fluted massive marble,
volcanic pink chalky dust, ghost grandparents

spitting black pits, picking their teeth.

PITCH

I left split-level houses extorted from the woods
in new New Jersey in July—birches, daisies,
leaves ripped by the thunder. My size 3's would

press a patch of tar molten in the constant sun
on their way to sharp and gleaming granite
curb that squared the end of the dead end.

When the black bubbling burst under my toe
the mystery of pitch infused my nose. With puffy
cheeks and wavy hair I could be Boreas, inflict

my spitting windy breath upon the world, the
cool breeze we all were dying for in humidity
woolly as the mammoths in La Brea.

My golden book of science held the mural
of dinosaurs in their world
where towered horns of ancient fern.

I walked beneath them. Treetops
dabbled light across the path, disappearing
cars and bases-loaded cheers.

EARTHLY MISHAPS

Faint, humming, inexorable in the damp
below the ruined walled castle garden
Mare's Tail tunnels an eight-foot root.

Sly-boots, I've spaded the circle, reached to my elbow.
Still the plant breaks. As Eve brought a man
his labor, it will multiply tenfold.

I shop for survival: a sprayer to level pride, melancholy
and unwanted shoots. The canister is lowered from
its shelf, bagged in plastic. The till rings.

Keys in hand, I see the carpark as a horsetracked swale
where Cadfael leads his roan, saddlebagged
with an apothecary box. Medieval herbicide?

As he stumps through mud, the monk's brass scale tips:
one pan sways with the bitterness of interrupted life,
the other, Eve's radical helplessness.

SATURDAY'S
prodigal feet

ABLE

We won the war
We sailed the seas
We burned the barren
We stormed the steeples

We aped the angels
We carved the carcass
We paged the peasant
We tamed the trees

We mocked the mother
We squared the circle
We moved the mountain
We primed the pump

We kicked the can
We bound the beast
We hailed the hero
We scaled the snake

We broke the breeze
We coined the coward
We drank the dregs
We left the lurch

We oiled the ocean
We arched the anguish
We rushed the river
We loved the lord

We crawled the chasm
We bore the burden
We fired the furnace
We sank the stars

We flew the flag
We won the war
Did you hear? the war
The war, did you hear?

CONTINENT, NOT COUNTRY

Instead of prayer I clean my teeth in Africa

after I buckle my chaps and lace up my boots,

bless earth on which I have no hangovers, bless paprika's

antibacterial float in the stomach where I've shoved the loot

of new potatoes and beef, parsley, leeks and crass

turnips they feed us at night before we watusi

our way across the trampled, bitten, sodden courtyard grass,

lift a leg across the horse's back, ride out, spelunkers

in a pitched pitch vault, the hooves' glint steely

with the ancient ambiguity of capture.

DESERT STORM

He keeps on touching her against the wall
beneath crucifix and candle, as blue silk
of the shade catches wick flaring white.

The red stub gutters. He's a waxy paraphrase.
At the edge of himself what he meets
is uncannily familiar, his plausible fiction.

The fire's light astride them—about, above, around—
he shifts her leg, her foot, off the ground.
The farther back she moves the further he swings.

OCCUPIED

Bruised ribs, raked shins
in the search for a sweet grape
among dry vines

Endlessly back and forth
reading maps, reading the legends:
'city of peace' 'gate of the gods'

Standing knee deep in the mud
of an untilled field
a rogue bull amid the red dirge

Hub of bricks on the flood plain
submerged save for its fame
Re-upped, streets radial from the gardens

Called again to prayer:
land of marshes and sand
looted and forced, and forced once more

Bone chips rattling
arms gone to a roadside bomb
Meat cold in the bowl

NOT YET EAGER TO STEP BACK FROM PUBLIC LIFE

Strikes against me out of the starting gate waiting

For the ball to drop none of your back talk cross

This line you die misguided deference to the honor

Code the deal is character leads to action at the drop

Of a hat bomb you back to the stone age taking the

First steps of a long journey expecting a greater

Voice in the party organization exacting detail to

Precipitate makeshift social revolution make again

Again yes we can with quantum computers develop

A groundswell and shoplift whatever's still here

FLOATS TO THE SKY

Initially I did not plan
    a painting of a ladder
        faithful to phantom
            noises before sleep

wearing a clean chemise
    beneath dirty shorts
        under a worn abaya
            in my pink slippers

with my red cheeks in the shop
    for spots of vitiligo
        and smoothing of their
            plump ragged history.

The canvas came bare
    as a bell before it's struck
        by brisk forced air
            on open waters

or the blue wasp
    that loved me
        when I was a child
            with a sting to the pineal

scattering bars through light
    all the way to dark
        faster than brush
            leaks down my hand.

TURNING IN TO THE
WINDSWEPT GARDEN

It's a messy sloppy business, this
immersion in samsara, the load
of murmurs twisting, out of joint.

In a heavy duty jacket against
the whipping air, the place called
home is just so small.

Struggle to the shrine. Face the calm
without benefit of baptism.
It's the left hand you must worry.

Consecrate impatience as spindrift
breaks into specks of shade. Lift
the missing limb over your mouth.

TRIBE

His charger trampling many a prickly star
Of sprouted thistle on the broken stones
—Tennyson's *Idylls*: Geraint, 313

I've patience with the black brow,
the marrow drained, bitter nurture,
now inherited wisdom is broken.

Sacral strife pokes from the heap,
a clavicle feuds with a rankle of ribs.
I sing no matins for the mess of bones.

They dug postholes bravely or cravenly
in famine or greed or self-defense
for terror and trouble. They built stockades

with hardwood and softwood, flame
haired bullies, polite quelled children
fed on cold butter, spent men.

FOR THE RECORD

All these years it's been in my head how psychology
relates to art the way a cigarette used to taste as we
slid about the earth—that turntable we wind up in.

In my prime on the street I danced a hymn to fire
as cloverleaf highways overtook truck farms
and oil storage tanks topped the estuaries.

My dance gained neither wing nor following
from one war to the next, sun today as bright
as moon last night, as my country reported
only its own losses. Stories of the ancients!

My tongue still pink, I ask for your help
in the brutal limbo of an afternoon
when a helpful stranger didn't shove me
aside from an oncoming car.

I cannot think what I was thinking, lying on
my back in the mercy of survival, blue heaven
cracked open on that road in neat red lines.

TRAFFIC

Walking toward the hotel
I press coins worth about five cents
into bumping hands.

These children's skulls are roasted
by hiphop and AIDS, bracketed
with begging one last stock of water.

The tiny clip-lit stage at the bar
features another small ragged form
paraded as *grande dame*.

Scantily-muscled Medea
sails into dark and damaged areas
with the cries of an ignited following.

Their screams do not disturb
a forefinger denting my chin.
I keep change in my hand as a passport.

MIRACLES WHEN THEY
ARE NEEDED

It was a way to eat in Periclean Athens and in nineteenth
century Paris and is now, where I sit disrobed
in an underheated room in Rockland County, subject

to the winks and chuckles of suburbanites who stopped
for drinks and kiss-the-wife and an exchange of business
suits for leisure wear before the weekly evening class.

Breathing and stretching, I rise from the pedestal,
step to the grey floor, stroke a foxtail brush, mix
pigments to set off the central figure on a canvas:

A commuter sways in the primitive john that empties
onto the tracks. Another swerves across the coupling
into the caboose (of German derivation, meaning a hut).

His fellow (toward the periphery) clambers to the cupola
where he will overlook the train's forward rush, the windows
static silver with momentum, *The Times*-screened profile

of a brisk CEO, dandruff flakes on padded shoulder. A flesh-
colored wad of gum flicked to the varnished center aisle awaits
the closure of a pick-up broom held by the naked sweeper.

The clock chimes, end of artists' break.
I drop brush as door pushes open to the musty room,
canvasses on easels near identical. They file in

in smocks, mustaches, goatees, cherooting their accomplishments,
expecting that my long legs will grace the platform, that my
body will be folded on the drapery's folds.

Fingers a fluid sweep as crowds murmur in my brain, on my way
out the door I purloin their supplies—watercolors, charcoal,
pastels. Years breathe by, my dimples disappear. My paintings

are presented. I cartoon my subjects, gesso my love
for them, wipe the turp rag on my need for them
—braggarts and don juans who can't sit still.

Passenger trains are shorter now. Crews walk freely
through the cars, rendering an inspection lookout obsolete.
The caboose has seen its day. I ready a frame

for the fish that bites the apostle back when the loaves
split twelve thousand ways into crumbs on the water where
a lone man walks. Rainbow oil rings surface on Galilee.

THE ENTIRE TABLE
LIFTED SPOONS

The voice need not smother words with articulated sound
Flamenco is all about pause, and curtains frayed

Lifting the leaf, momentarily
Rubbing lemon juice into the unfolded paper for the message

We may hang our pots instead of shelving them
But we'll go the way of our grandmothers

There is deep sad sighing, all grief and complaint
The texture of one summer afternoon after another

Next, please, the lady in pink
And the rainbow's brighter end, paler span

Somewhere ribbons burst the wrappings of a present
And a statue pats the air

CROWS WITHOUT A BARDO

Their calls louder than the day itself
would deafen the moment of death.
A tree of water in the center arcs translucent
branches, pelts its buds, stimulates their
pin feather blood. They are murdering the bowl
in the double decker fountain.

Staccato overlays any time between lives, their wing
span night. Their beaks wrap any past life—
for their disputes are harmonies, their possession
of the fountain supreme. Discordant brown wet mulch
bedding thirsty annuals below the fountain's lip
cannot hold. A two-storied covered wagon—
the plaza of shops sets off into the world.

A lead crow perches, fills my good ear:
This train rolls, to desert or to coast, more
to come than anyone expects,
stops for a bicentennial, infinite
auditory delusions, dawn's early light.
We are hooped! don't trust the old ruts!

I open the parenthesis, climb down.
A black cat crosses the path. The wagon
backs up, lets me by—to take the blues.

LINCOLN IN ANOTHER BARDO

If aluminum foil hadn't more glints
a crow would lift me up for nesting matter.
There's an off chance she might pilfer me for
crowning ornament: one less loose copper.

Copper I am, not iron, though a long ways
from the silver tongue of thy prophets.
I shine in the footsteps of passersby.
I shine small and round and presidential.

Do you see me slow to anger, gracious
and merciful, abiding in steadfast love?
You would seem to be addressing
old envelopes stamped with my visage.

Games and prizes, land and research
have waylaid your prodigal feet.
I don't want to hold you up. But I do.
The arc of history could bend with you.

SWARMING

Long stitches—the wild bees seam
their rumpled pouch
in the tree trunk's hollow

Five-petaled berry flowers
then peach nubs
pump the days

What happens hereafter
could be perpetual learning
Compost draws flies, snakes slither

Let's ask for lemon with tea
before honey
Before it's hemmed

NEWBIE

I'm waiting for the bus
      sack on indelible back
            the last straw of alfalfa
                  tickling epiglottis

my nylon raincoat
      drenched and heavy
            as a cassock, world
                  a shooter marble

up against my small one.
      Serenity rises in the
            east but doesn't
                  end at this stop.

We are steps away
      from a fitness center, and
            you know humans:
                  when we leave

someplace, or someone
      an undetectable
            viral load persists—
                  committed to memory

under the green lindens—
      the dachsund or the badger?
            patriot or traitor?
                  a trial or a thrill?

A BRUSH WITH CONTUMACY

The landscape painter swats the river
distracted by a swarm of gnats
clambering the muddy bank.

Schoolchildren balance on the peeling log
lurching, vainly grabbing a zigzag across stormcloud.

Momentarily, a migratory blue
alights on still-damp opaque white.

Molting petals from a spent magnolia
wrinkle the siena backs of mothers lazing by the water.

Gone girl! where's that steady hand
for brushing in the twittering sparrows
hooking sparrowhawk?

EMBER DAYS

The almanac's laconic whistle
passes a millennium at last grown
nonfungible. Day breaks up the where-were-

you party. Feet wander concrete platforms
lit with radiance weak and discomfited
from two bare bulbs, stilled double-naughts.

Mobiles dry-rattle beneath posters for stewpots
and holiday sales, the forecast troubled music:
history, or at least cold wind of a startling event.

A cricket's chirrup slows to intermittent pipe.
Hooves break the dried railside bramble. Auburn
summer coats thickened gray, the fawns cluck.

TAKEN

Seven years it took me to untangle
the vow I made before I ever met you
to not slip to a bedroom down the hall
from the way I felt beside you at the Mahler
after knowing you five days, and then two nights away.

Early at the track. I'd missed the train,
clocks sprung by summertime. I had to take in
Exsultate Jubilate standing at the foyer video.

Across the wynds that night snow fell, melted
the next day. The next month, home, freeze-
framed in my marriage bed, out on the street
twa corbies beaked a flattened squirrel.

The years have rinsed my straitened cells, developed
our art's aim: to reveal the life we live as it effaces
your shutter capturing my shadow on a lawn.

A— uses more ordnance in a single campaign than B— used in epochs of imperial rule

May you not be subjected to civilizing missions

May you want to continue more than you want to stop

May God move your muscles as you lie there

May you be passed over by the local police

May God spare you the mornings of steady heat

May your computers learn to make the dead talk

May no one stop your ears to the bee-hum

May none indulge in witty banter before the eerie video clip

May God roll in, the fog in the first cool hour

May your weeping with remembrance be in slippers

May you be forcible within your heart

May your fertile regions not be barbarized, nor your large populations

May you dine in restaurants and work in offices

May the light enlarge thy days

May God occupy thy country

ACKNOWLEDGMENTS

Grateful acknowledgment is made to the editors of the following publications, in which some of these poems first appeared, sometimes in slightly different form: *Barrow Street, Fence, The Fiddlehead, Hotel Amerika, Interim: A Journal of Poetry & Poetics, Matter: A Journal of Political Poetry and Commentary, Notre Dame Review, Passages North, Persimmon Tree, Seneca Review, Slant: A Journal of Poetry, Smartish Pace, Stand, Stone Canoe, TAB: A Journal of Poetry and Poetics, Tampa Review, Vallum, The Woven Tale Press.*

A number of these poems appeared in *The Ruined Walled Castle Garden* (2020), winner of the Bright Hill Press Poetry Chapbook Competition.

'Infinitives' was shortlisted by *Aesthetica Magazine* and is anthologized in *Aesthetica Creative Writing Award 2023*.

'Ember Days' is anthologized in *NDR's Milestone 50: The Anniversary Issue* (2021).

'Able,' and 'Lincoln in Another Bardo' are among a set of poems awarded 1st Prize in Poetry in the 2023 International Literary Seminars (ILS)/*Fence* Contest.

My thanks to Millay Arts for my second-ever juried residency and its gifts of space and time. And something more: As I slept on my good ear, other fellows in The Barn heard walking upstairs in my studio; in the morning, I would find the lights on. I was a newly-minted Chödma and we picked a concentration-time for all while I did a practice in my studio to clear their anxiety and calm the disturbance. Millay, thank you too for deep snow steps uphill after blizzard!

NOTES OF GRATITUDE TO...

Offering the Body: The Tibetan Practice of Chöd...root teacher Chögyal Namkhai Norbu for 1992 transmission of Dzogchen secondary practices.........**Infinitives**... writing students in "Ecosystems & Ego Systems" spring 2006 at Cornell's medical college in Doha while US military operations caused suffering and pollution across the Gulf.........**Outside The Tunnel Snow Is Melting**... photographer Richard Henley and his staircase in Mill Valley.........**Excuse Me Hello Good Morning Good Night**... Sister Timothy Marie, OP, and her precise instruction in earth science and biology.........**Up With People**...Mary Beth O'Connor who was actually on that TV show......... **As Though Finny Folk Would Flip**...Deanna Bodnar who said the fish's name.........**There Is No Known Remedy For Scale**...Radionics practitioner Maj. Kate Hopwood Payne for the poem's title.........**Is a transcendently beautiful place not to be ours?**...Asbury Sallenger's *Island in a Storm* which includes Emma Mille's story......**Blossoms Burst Every-which Color**...Ron Schoneman for line 1 in exchange for pulmonaria, Jen Skala for line 2 spoken during our collaborating with nature.........**Pat Euphoria**...photography innovator, photojournalist, and World War II correspondent Lee Miller (1907 - 1977) who had one exhibit during her lifetime....Drue Heinz for complimentary tickets for Hawthornden 2001 residents to her second, the retrospective in Edinburgh.........**I Am The Blond You Wanted**...Ned Delaney for talks and walks and then some.........**Dry Dock**... college buddies Ann Woodward on North campus and Ken McClane on West.........**To The Darkhouse**...literary genius Virginia Woolf who drowned herself in the River Ouse in the spring of 1941.........**Tesla On A Leash**...Nikola Tesla (1856 - 1943), electrical engineer, physicist and inventor, who discovered alternating current.........**Earthly Mishaps**...

Rosslyn's overgrown garden.........**Able**...Allen Ginsberg for well-timed words about a topic missing from this poem's draft.........**Continent Not Country**...the 54 now independent countries that comprise 1 of the earth's continents......... **Desert Storm** and **Occupied**...the dead, the damaged, the bereaved, the plants and animals, the air, water, land......... **Miracles When They Are Needed**...painter Mark Rothko for his prose piece from whence the poem's title....The Guerrilla Girls' 1989 poster on New York City buses: "Do women have to be naked to/ get into the Met. Museum? //Less than 5% of the artists in the Modern/ Art Sections are women, but 85%/ of the nudes are female".........**Crows Without A Bardo**... Susan Gardner for the 2019 Red Mountain residency on Sanibel Island whereon the fountain was.........**Ember Days**... Alison Lurie, who on a first reading felt the train pulling out of London, for winter writing days on Hanshaw Road......... **Taken**...Robin Robertson for sharing the castle.........*A— uses more ordnance in a single campaign than B— used in epochs of imperial rule*...David C. Hendrickson's "The Curious Case of American Hegemony" in *World Policy Journal* from which the poem's title is adapted

ABOUT THE AUTHOR

Mary Gilliland is author of two award-winning poetry collections: *The Devil's Fools* and *The Ruined Walled Castle Garden*. Her work has been anthologized most recently in *Rumors Secrets & Lies: Poems on Pregnancy, Abortion & Choice,* and *Wild Gods: The Ecstatic in Contemporary Poetry and Prose*. After college Mary apprenticed with Gary Snyder in the Sierra foothills where she studied Buddhism and helped to build a wood-framed public school. She's received the Stanley Kunitz Fellowship from the Fine Arts Work Center and a Council on the Arts Faculty Grant from Cornell University where she was instrumental in developing the Knight Institute for Writing.

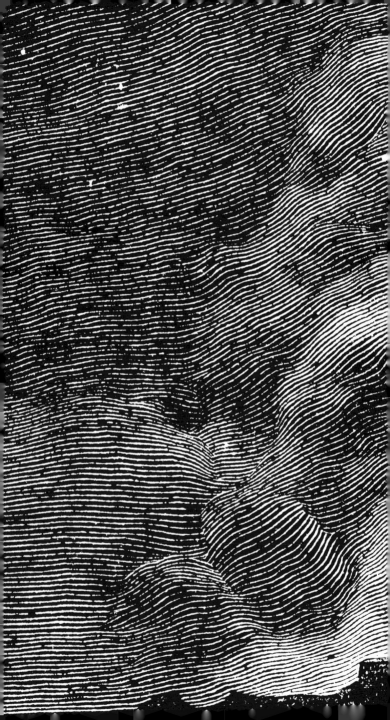